101 USES FOR
AN EX-HUSBAND

101 USES FOR AN EX-HUSBAND

RICHARD SMITH

CARTOONS BY DEBRA SOLOMON

WARNER BOOKS

A Time Warner Company

Copyright © 1997 by Richard Smith
Cartoons copyright © 1997 by Debra Solomon

All rights reserved.

Warner Books, Inc., 1271 Avenue of the Americas, New York, NY 10020

Visit our Web site at http://pathfinder.com/twep

W A Time Warner Company

Printed in the United States of America

First Printing: August 1997

10 9 8 7 6 5 4 3 2 1

ISBN: 0-446-67372-2
LC: 97-60617

Book design and text composition by H. Roberts Design
Cover concept and design by Diane Luger
Cover photograph by Ann Stratton

For L.B., my favorite ex-wife

Acknowledgments

Our thanks to the hundreds of ex-wives who flooded us with suggestions, some tasteful and many, frankly, quite shocking. Also, owing to state laws, we included only those uses that do not violate community standards.

Introduction

The end of a marriage or lengthy relationship can be one of life's great traumas, like the loss of a pet, or flying standby to Altoona. Yet, just as with the flu or a run in your best pantyhose, you get over it. Studies, in fact, show that 96 out of 100 women who experience such a loss go on either to a better, more romantic relationship or their master's in business.

Ex-husbands and ex-boyfriends, of course, come in a variety of shapes and sizes. Yours may be a vile creep over whom you wouldn't shed a tear if to pay alimony he had to moonlight as a crash dummy. Or maybe he isn't so bad, an amiable but boring little man to whom you'd cheerfully send a get-well card if, while ice fishing, he fell through the ice and got neutered by a passing barracuda. He may even be a terrific guy who, when the smoke clears, will make a great friend, especially if he has a strong back and you need a sofa carried up four flights of stairs.

Depending on how angry you are, we're certain you've already thought of several uses for your ex, many wicked, some unlawful (example: marinating your ex in kerosene, then using him as a space heater), the best ones, perhaps, devised over a pitcher of sangria while you lunched with a creative friend unhampered by a conscience. For women whose imagination is temporarily incapacitated, however, this book offers a range of satisfying suggestions. When trained to lie still, for instance, a dumpy ex with ample body fat makes a soft, comfy footstool. Paint him the right color, and a porky ex becomes a conversation-starting doorstop. Love to read? Use a skinny ex as a bookmark or, at holiday time, tie a little bow around his head and use him as a last-minute stocking stuffer for a girl friend seeking a New Year's Eve date (some assembly may be required).

To facilitate your task, we've divided this book into what researchers call the Three Stages of Separation: 1. When You Want Him Dead. 2. When You Merely Loathe Him. 3. When Enough Time Has Passed So You Can Actually Stand the Sight of Him.

A fourth stage—Gloating Because He Left You for a Sex-Crazed Little Trollop Who's Already Given Him Two Heart Attacks in One Night—is in preparation.

Note: To further assist you, we've included throughout the book several end-of-relationship questions even the most experienced divorce attorney may not be able to answer. We hope you find our answers, all painstakingly researched, helpful.

Part I

When You Want Him Dead

*A*t this stage your anger is, understandably, extreme. Even the most loving, caring, and compassionate woman may be shocked to find herself smiling, even giggling, as she imagines her ex as a surface-to-air missile—the poor guy either a skeet target or, if she prefers him crispy, the first man on the sun. One woman reported getting intense satisfaction when she pictured her ex-husband smoking in bed while wearing her Valentine's Day gift: flammable pajamas. Another woman, mildly depressed because her husband had left her for his secretary, actually grew euphoric while imagining her narcissistic ex, the possessor of a huge ego, the center of attention at an autopsy. (One profoundly sensitive divorcée made mention of teensy guilt pangs when she envisioned her ex, an extreme-sports addict, inadvertently bungee jumping into a large vat of camel waste. Happily, however, it didn't ruin her evening.)

In this first section, because we offer several PG-rated uses, women of delicate constitution—even if they're victims of a contemptible ex—may feel just a tad guilty should they find themselves laughing out loud. No need to worry; this is normal.

Yule Log

5

Shrunken Head

Asbestos Remover

Ashtray

First Man to Almost Swim the Bering Strait

Bonus Use—Channeling Your Anger Productively

Sadistic? Perhaps. But if you're especially incensed because he left you for, say, a younger woman, consider the following everyday uses for your ex:

1. When suitably coated and baked: Anatomically correct gingerbread man
2. When suitably decomposed: Compost (for your new vegetable garden)
3. When suitably mounted: Hobbyhorse

Note: Two uses* if he left you for a younger man:

- Castration (by guillotine if he's French). Reconsider, however, if there's the slightest chance that you might marry him again.

- Acupuncture circumcision (ever so satisfying when performed without anesthesia)

---

* Not technically uses, but nevertheless cathartic if you're still cross with him.

The First Man on the Sun

Pincushion

Drano Taster

13

Official Ex-Wife First Aid Kit

The Essentials

- Lots of soft hankies or box of fluffy tissues to dab away tears of joy that he's finally out of your life (a not atypical reaction by women who were married to men who eat dinner in their underwear)

- Phone number of a marvelous divorce attorney*

- Aspirin (or Tylenol if your stomach is sensitive), to relieve Lawyer Headache, the primary symptom of which is the feeling that the hourly fee is outrageous

- Ice cream (an FDA-approved over-the-counter tranquilizer)

- Lots of take-out menus (Pamper yourself. For now, it's okay to let strangers cook for you.)

- One old, patched baby blanket (provides instant stress relief when gently rubbed against side of face)

- Stuffed teddy bear (generic male substitute—use for snuggling and kissing goodnight, and he won't get jealous if you bring home a date)

- Travel agent (A change of scene speeds the recovery process. Try the all-inclusive singles package to Machu Picchu or the Get-Away-from-It-All Club Med weekend in Kalamazoo.)

*One who returns your phone call within three days.

- Fireplace (Gazing into a crackling fire while slowly sipping a decent burgundy—a '93 Chambertin, for instance—will help you contemplate a brighter, happier future.)

- Mace (in case your neighbor's husband starts hitting on you)

Also Nice to Have

- Shot put (for playing dodgeball with your ex. Caution: May leave marks.)

- Smelling salts (should you discover your ex is going out with your best friend)

- Slim volume of Shakespeare sonnets (accelerates the healing process when read by candlelight while you soak in a warm bath)

- A furry, purry nonjudgemental cat who sits in your lap and stares adoringly into your eyes (Or, if you're allergic to cat hair, borrow a dog who licks your face.)

- A girl friend who loves you unconditionally (i.e., will take your 3:24 A.M. calls without asking, "Do you know what *time* it is?")

- Brewer's yeast (prevents pre-blind-date fluid retention)

- Amulet (to ward off The Spirit of Husband Past during intimate moments with a new man)

- A veil (for drama when you visit your lawyer)

Stress Reducer

Shark Bait

Richard Smith

Q: When out with friends, how bubbly should I be? Happy face? Sad face? Or what?

A: As a rule, the degree of public effervescence should be directly proportional to how you feel inside (good role models: Greta Garbo in Camille or Nixon leaving the White House). You don't want to appear too jolly, of course; friends may be shocked. We suggest affecting a sort of melancholic beauty-enhancing demeanor (light application of jojoba moisture cream, accentuate with purple eyeliner, just a hint of rouge—gives a nice tragically sorrowful effect, much like the face of someone who's just swallowed a moth).

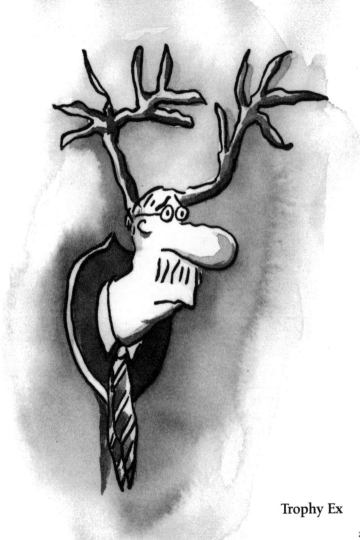

Trophy Ex

Medical Model

The First Man Over Niagara Falls in a Yachting Cap

Q: What if I run into my ex in a restaurant and he's with a beautiful leggy blonde? Do I ignore or acknowledge him?

A: <u>SMILE WARMLY AND SHAKE HIS HAND IF:</u>

You're with an incredible hunk (killer pecs, thick-pile hair, devastating smile, pearly teeth, cleft chin, deep Walter Cronkite voice, mysterious patch ever one eye).

You feel detached, serene, in total control. You wonder: What did I ever see in him? Did he always have such enormous pores? Is his jawline . . . well . . . not to be unkind, but . . . is it growing less firm? And, oh God! Is that the beginning of a paunch?

<u>RUN THE OTHER WAY IF:</u>

You're with the blind date from Dork World: 5'3", pudgy, major razor burn, teeth like Stonehenge, wearing 6 gold chains, keeps staring at the dessert cart and drooling.

Your knees turn to marmalade, your pulse spikes to 160, the pit of your stomach feels like you've just eaten tainted shellfish, and you're starting to lose just the tiniest bit of bladder control.

SMILE WARMLY AND SHAKE HIS HAND IF:

Daily workouts and a l0-pound weight loss have conferred upon you Goddess-Plus status. Your flawless tan, silky hair, and copious use of teeth whiteners make you look extradelicious and radiant. (**Beauty tip:** Write to Hillary R. Clinton for her free pamphlet, "Controlling the Frizzies in 30 Days or Less.")

RUN THE OTHER WAY IF:

Today is the day:

- Your skin is blotchy.
- A hungover hairdresser decided you need bangs.
- You chipped a nail.
- A long-dormant zit has finally erupted.
- There are dark circles under your eyes.
- Your upper-lip depilatory has failed utterly.

Soup Thickener

24

Elvis Impersonator

Roadkill

Official Ex-Wife To-Do List

Admittedly, disposing of an ex's belongings is a chore, but definitely worthwhile—think of all that extra closet and drawer space. Some suggestions:

ITEM	DISPOSITION
HIS CUFF LINKS (CHEAP)	Flush down toilet
(EXPENSIVE)	Melt down; convert precious metal into the tennis bracelet you've always wanted
MUTUAL FRIENDS	Keep good ones; donate losers to charity
PORNO TAPES	See above
HOUSE	Keep
PAINSTAKINGLY ASSEMBLED COLLECTION OF SUPER-RARE BASEBALL CARDS	Line bottom of birdcage or give to teething toddler
PIAGET WATCH	Pawn; use cash for therapeutic trip to Cancún. Bask in sun, obtain glorious, beauty-enhancing tan
EXPENSIVE GOLF CLUBS OR SKIS	Spring planting. Insert in ground; use to support tomato vines
12 IRREPLACEABLE BOTTLES OF CHÂTEAU LATOUR 1948	Juggling practice, or donate to Meals on Wheels
BOX OF AGED CUBAN MONTECRISTOS	Office grab bag, or smoke them with a girlfriend
HIS MISTRESS	Dumpster

ITEM	DISPOSITION
CLOTHING:	
TIES (CHEAP)	Burn, place ashes in memorial urn
(EXPENSIVE)	Use as birthday gifts should next boyfriend have the same neck size (Waste not, want not)
GUCCI BELTS	Tie-backs for drapes
CALVIN KLEIN SUITS	Either: 1. Slice off sleeves then return to ex via Parcel Post, or 2. display on lawn, sell for $1.00 each
ARMANI CASHMERE BLAZER	Fold carefully; use as soft cushiony bed for elderly incontinent cat
SOCKS	Dusting plant leaves
SHOES (RUNNING)	Smacking cockroaches
(BRUNO MAGLI)	Planters for amaryllis bulbs
JOINT BANK ACCOUNT	1. Run to bank. 2. Close account. 3. Place cash and bottle of Champagne in safety deposit box. 4. Celebrate with cute vault guard when divorce becomes final
HIS PRICELESS BEATLES LPs	Frisbees or coasters
STAIRMASTER, STATIONARY BIKE, TREADMILL	Keep. Use to trim those few odd pounds, firm thighs, tighten already curvaceous butt; look maddeningly luscious, meet dreamy new man

Food Taster

29

Sword Swallower

Landfill

Teething Ring

Christmas Ornament

Party Snack

Tag Sale

Compost

Unsuccessful Escape Artist

Post Breakup Recovery Table

How long until you feel like your old, happy self? According to experts, the rule of thumb for an emotionally mature woman with high self-esteem (a feisty heavy equipment operator or a carrier pilot) is one month for each year you were together. Less secure women (victims of either too much tofu or too little fettucine Alfredo) may take a bit longer, as noted below.

IF YOU WERE MARRIED FOR	YOU'LL ACHIEVE TOTAL RECOVERY[1] IN
3 months	1 week[2]
7 months to 2 years	2 months[3]
3 to 5 years	6 months[4]
6 to 10 years	8 months[5]
11 or more years	1 year[6]

1. Clinicians define "total recovery" as the ability to hear "Our Song" on your car radio without driving into a guardrail.
2. Only 15 minutes if he lets you keep the wedding gifts.
3. 4 minutes, 13 seconds if he calls to tell you that he thinks he made a big mistake. Make him grovel.
4. During this period try not to mope; it causes crows' feet.
5. Just 8 days if you're still a virgin.
6. 2 years if you're still having sex with him.*

* Not recommended if you've remarried another man.

Speed Bump

39

Mummy

Organ Donor

41

Part II

When You Merely Loathe Him

On second thought, why end his suffering? Death is too good for him—and think of all that paperwork. Now that you only despise him, let your imagination run wild. You are, of course, above such ghastly thoughts as your ex's parachute failing while skydiving or, during a trek through the Andes, your ex being carried off as an hors d'oeuvre by a famished condor. Consider, however: Is he an avid gardener? Place him on his back, affix a hose to his navel, pry open his mouth, and presto! the neighbors will love your new lawn sprinkler. Are you taking a gourmet cooking class? Perfect. Insert your ex headfirst into your roast, and voilà! He's a hi-tech meat thermometer who chirps when the lamb is done. What about his quirks: Is he rigid? Lucky you! Simply lay him flat, balance him on a central support, and you've got a one-of-a-kind seesaw. And if he's thick-skulled and bald, be practical: Sharpen your kitchen knives on the side of his head.

Target Practice

Bedpan

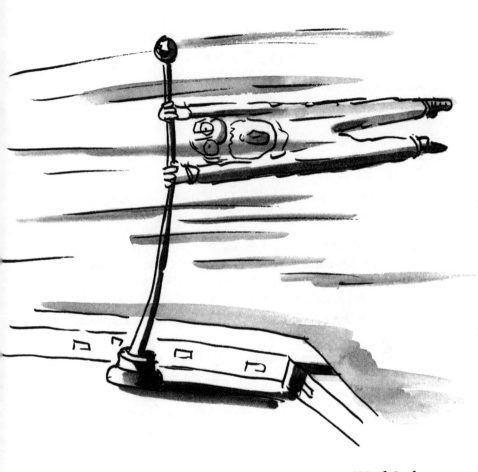

Wind Sock

Richard Smith

Bonus Use—Turn a Corrupt Ex-Husband Into a Cash Cow

See actual fax below, which, in slightly altered form, netted one ex-wife nearly $11,000.

Memo to: Internal Revenue Service

From: Wronged Woman

Re: Receipt of generous reward from the IRS for turning in a lying little tax cheat and pervert. (No, I'm not hostile.)

Dear IRS Auditor:

I'm no snitch, but as a concerned citizen-patriot, I think there are things about my ex-husband you ought to know.

Unreported income? Don't get me started. Let's start with payoffs for looking the other way when defense contractors charge $633.89 for a toilet and $750.29 for the seat.

Also allow me to mention trips with his secretary to Paris, London, and Hilton Head he's been claiming as (don't make me laugh) business expenses. And check it out: That $10,000 charitable deduction to United Way? Note the puddle under his chair when you demand the receipt and canceled check. Oh, and don't be bashful: Ask him how, on $40,000 a year, he bought that new Mercedes parked in his driveway.

Fire Hydrant

Fabric Softener

Wind Chime

Chimney Sweep

Q: How soon should I start dating?

A: Some women, if there's nothing good on television, begin dating the night of the breakup. We suggest, however, waiting at least 24 hours; you still may be in shock. When you're finally ready, treat yourself to one of those recreational males (body of a hunk, IQ of a tree frog, also known as a Mr. Right-Now), like a lifeguard with to-die-for buns or a personal trainer named Rolf. A ski instructor with washboard abs and a monster mane of blond hair is also good.*

Q: Must these men be intelligent?

A: No, just built, reasonably amusing, and not inclined to feel hurt because you ask for the abridged version when they start telling you about their day. It also helps if they hold advanced degrees in baby oil massages and loofah management.

* For more information, call our exclusive Emergency Hotline: 1-800 BOY TOYS.

Guard Dog

Q: Are singles bars a good idea?

A: Yes, especially if they feature free munchies. Even if you don't meet a lovely man, it will perk up your ego to be asked for your number, and there's always the chance that a man of quality* will wander in. Avoid strange men, however, who approach you with any of the following lines:

1. "Hold me tight; I just need some closeness."
2. "I'm not sure I can love again."
3. "I'd be nothing without you." (He's desperate.)
4. "I'm not sure I can be with a woman like you."
5. "My mother would really like you."
6. "I think there's something kind of . . . well . . . beautiful about the word 'boilermaker.'"

---

* Knows what a fish fork's for.

Noninvasive Liposuction

Mailbox

Bonus Use—Negative Role Model

So you don't make the same mistake twice: Let your ex exemplify the qualities you don't want in the next man you get involved with. Do you really, after all, want yet another partner who:

- Fails to notice when you've lost 5 pounds.

- Opens the car door for you, but only when it's moving.

- During sex, calls out his own name.

- Smacks his lips when he eats chicken salad.

- Lacks a hairy chest to snuggle against on cold nights.

- Would rather hold the TV clicker than your hand.

- At dinner parties, makes calls on his cellular.

- Remembers to put the seat down only when you're sitting on it.

Pooper Scooper

Beekeeper

Mr. Potato Head

Richard Smith

Bonus Use—Party Animal

A former husband with a sense of humor makes a great entertainment provider. When friends are over and you happen to have a spare box of carpet tacks, amuse yourselves by playing Pin the Tail on the Ex.* The winner (the player who scores the most exit wounds) gets to point him in the direction of the Band-Aids.

*For best results, ask ex not to flinch.

Satellite Dish

65

Rolling Pin

Bonus Use—Muse for Your Angry Roman à Clef

Suggested title: *Men Are From Mars; Why Don't They Stay There?*

Sample Chapter VII—An Innocent Wife Discovers That Things Aren't Always What They Seem to Be

During the year, Brittany, a sweet, lovely, giving, caring, warm, compassionate midlevel manager for a large corporation, often found items of lingerie from Victoria's Secret in her husband's glove compartment. Ever trusting, however, she assumed they belonged to Adolf, their kinky Porsche mechanic. It was after Clyde said he had to work late at the office on Thanksgiving, Chanukah, Christmas Eve, and New Year's Eve, then always took a shower the *instant* he got home (which didn't work; the little rat still reeked of Shalimar) that Brittany began to grow suspicious. "I may be naive," she thought, tears welling in her lovely emerald-green eyes, "but I'm no fool." She took a deep breath, threw back her shoulders, and strapped on her shoulder holster. It was time to confront Clyde.

Sunscreen

Meat Thermometer

Bonus Use—Pen Pal

Is he behind with alimony? Child support? Our direct marketing consultant designed the following result-getting letter. It is particularly effective when signed in blood.

Dear Microbe:

You're way behind with your child support and alimony payments. I'm not going to sue; you know how I hate courtrooms—tacky ambience, no smoking, Domino's doesn't deliver, etc.—but if you and that dreary tart you moved in with want to live to see next week, you will FedEx a cashier's check in the amount of $ _____ plus an extra $ _____ (10% late payment penalty) by _____. Have a nice day.

Note: For quicker results, instead of mailing, E-mail your message to his office. His co-workers will love it.

Bird Feeder

Kibble Bit

Bonus Use—Inspiration for Your Very Own Web Site

Caution: The following sites already exist:

- http://www/ngi.net/A Betrayed Woman's Chat Room.com

- whoa://www.ow/Can't-Fail Hexes For Hateful Exes.oh

- www.com./Boy, Have I suffered.com

- told://you/so/Mom Was Right.com

- httm://www/Ruin The S.O.B.//com

- httm://Marriage for Beginners.//com

- oops://Avoid Lawyers who wear garters.//ow

Paintbrush

Top

Chia Pet

Bonus Use—Allow Memories of Your Ex-Husband to Inspire You When Stuck for Good Scrabble Words.

A FEW SUGGESTIONS:

Nine nouns:
1. TOAD
2. SCUM
3. SLEAZEBALL
4. TWERP
5. PIG (or SWINE)
6. TROGLODYTE (VERMIN okay if you have no T's)
7. CHEAT
8. SHOE
9. FETISH

Five adjectives:
1. SELFISH
2. ROTTEN
3. FILTHY
4. SLIMY
5. SLEAZY (if you don't have enough letters to spell SLEAZEBALL)

Two adverbs:
1. LIMPLY
2. IMPOTENTLY

Bonus Use—When Selecting Vanity Plates for Your New Vehicle, Let Your Ex Be the Role Model

SIX PLATES OFTEN REQUESTED BY EX-WIVES:

1. WED 2 1 PUTZ
2. X A SIKE O
3. NO 4 PLAY
4. PP (if he's a bed wetter)
5. X A D V ANT
6. BOUGHT WITH DIVORCE SETTLEMENT
   (for residents of states with wraparound license plates only)

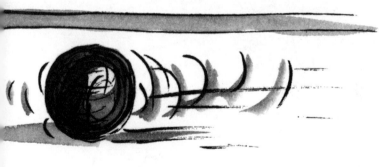

Bowling Pin

Lab Rat

Golf Tee

Bonus Use—Guinea Pig

Want to impress the new man in your life with your culinary expertise? Use an ex with a sensative stomach to try out your risotto primavera or, for something more manly, that gourmet recipe for pork hocks in wine sauce* you found while sitting in your dentist's office flipping through the pages of *Mercenary*. If he doesn't double over or plead for a laxative, you know it's a perfect dish to serve your new lover.

*Use leftovers for a romantic breakfast in bed.

Part III

When Enough Time Has Passed So You Can Actually Stand the Sight of Him

*Y*ou're beginning to heal. You've calmed down, and, being the sane, rational, practical person that you are, you realize that the little geek may actually come in handy. You may even be on speaking terms, which gives you the right, if you're squeamish, to ask him to come over and remove the dead squirrel in your driveway. Thinking of dating again? Ask your ex for a reference. Or perhaps he has nanny potential; ask him to take the cats for the weekend so you and your new boyfriend can spend a few days in Vail. If your ex has an oily complexion, you might even consider sticking a little wick in his head and using him as a reading candle. And, if he still cares about you, he'll be more than happy to chaperone in case you have misgivings about going on a blind date with a man sentenced to 400 hours of community service.

Tip: If you still harbor resentment toward an exceptionally odious ex (the type who indicates he's feeling amorous by crushing beer cans against his head) and he's a gun nut, one ex-wife suggested making him weep by giving his new assault rifle a bubble bath.

Reading Lamp

War Memorial

Bonus Use—Trade-In

Ex-Wife Swap Meets (see "Pre-Owned Men" in the classified section of your local paper) provide ample opportunity to exchange your old used-up ex for a newer, low-mileage husband—one who understands you, worships you, remembers your birthday, and instantly responds to your frantic elbow jabs when he snores.

Tip: Be sure that new special someone comes with the standard New Man Warranty: 20 dates or 20 meals, whichever comes first.

Stepstool

Shower Caddy

Bungee Cord

Bonus Use—Visiting Nurse Service

When your mother's out of town, a sensitive ex* can be an ideal health care provider. Head stuffy? Running a fever? Throat sore? Too ill to get out of bed? Sick of watching *Flintstones* reruns? Call and invite him to make a house call. Remind him to bring:

- The current *TV Guide*

- A vaporizer

- An over-the-counter restorative (preferably chicken soup)

- Aerosol disinfectant spray (you don't want to catch whatever he might have)

- Nyquil (or an approved substitute such as herbal tea or, if your fever's really up, cognac)

- A jar of Smucker's Raspberry Jam (for bedsores)

- A dietary supplement to help you heal faster (like chocolate chip cookies or Fig Newtons)

- Buffalo wings (to fortify the immune system)

- A coloring book and crayons

Etiquette tip: So he doesn't get the wrong idea, dismiss him the moment you're feeling better.

* One who either a) can't stand human suffering or b) is guilt-ridden.

Pull Toy

Garlic Press

Hammock

Coatrack

Leaf Blower

Bonus Use—Excuse to Get Rid of the Pest Who Keeps Calling

Did you give your phone number to a psycho poet during a rash moment? Were you slightly tipsy when you agreed to date the needy dentist who came on to you at the gallery opening? Use your ex to diplomatically dump Mr. Wrong. Send him a brief note explaining: "Dear Marvin, You're a really special person and I loved meeting Sue, your truck, but my ex-husband and I are getting back together. This time we're really going to make our marriage work (keep your fingers crossed). We've joined the Peace Corps. By the time you get this, we'll be helping the locals dig a well in Ethiopia. Try not to hate me."

Note: If you're out of stamps, just leave a brief message on his answering machine ("Hi Marv, I'm out of here, bye.")

Tip: In the future, refrain from letting men without references buy you drinks at those Parents Without Partners singles mixers.)

Travel Companion

Room Divider

Q: Just in case—How do I get through trying moments?

A: You could consult one of those "psychic friends," but they generally have more problems than you need. Instead, either read the Bible (Luke, John, and Proverbs are extra-comforting and don't have lots of verbs ending in "eth") or switch to fourth-stage thinking and recall your ex's drawbacks:

- He never appreciated your witty remarks.

- He moved his lips when he read *Hustler*.

- He never wanted to go anywhere.

- He criticized you in front of others.

- He looked moronic in a Santa costume.

- That cool ponytail turned out to be his brain stem.

- He had a nervous tendency, when stopped for speeding, to expel gas.

Bongo Drum

Pepper Grinder

Bonus Use—Protect Your Home During Electrical Storms

If he's not afraid of heights, an ex:

1. With a long neck,
2. And his arms extended upward,
3. Wearing a copper derby,
4. Securely affixed to your roof

makes an inexpensive but highly effective lightning rod.*

---

*Or, during clement weather, use a mallet and a wrench to convert your ex into a weather vane.

Silent Butler

Sex Toy

Lectern

Q: Suppose I go to a party and meet a man. How do I tell if he has Mr. Right potential?

A: Rely on your instinct, that inner gut reaction that tells you either to a) continue chatting—this guy sounds neat, or b) excuse yourself, go into the bedroom with a bottle of vodka, and lie down on the coats. The answer to your question also can be expressed by Veldbein's Third Law of Male Neediness:

$$SA = \frac{Ncf}{m.p.h. \times CD}$$

in which SA (how starved he is for affection) equals Ncf (number of little cocktail franks he eats with a toothpick in 5 minutes) divided by m.p.h. (how fast he chews them) multiplied by CD (the cost of the dress you bought to wear to this party).

Ironing Board

Tennis Net

Hassock

Sundial

Mousetrap

Q: When I'm finally feeling better, will there be any lasting damage?

A: Highly unlikely. In fact, CAT scans of recently de-partnered women show that even the most traumatic breakup affects only that portion of the brain used to follow the plot line of Days of Our Lives and sing karaoke.

Q: For my next relationship, what kind of man should I look for?

A: A terrific one. The rules are simple. Avoid any man who:

1. Can't pass: a) an insurance physical and b) a credit check.
2. Has dinner with his mother once a week, rain or shine.
3. On your first dinner date, obsessively talks about his ex-wife while frantically rolling bread pellets between his fingers (suggests latent psychosis; get out of there).
4. Has been "between careers" since 1989.
5. Goes to work wearing a ski mask.
6. Thinks safe sex means drawing the blinds.
7. Turns ashen and grinds his teeth when you mention the word *commitment*.
8. Is too insecure about his manhood to tell you, "No problem, sweetie," when you ask him to pick up a box of tampons on his way home from the rifle range.
9. Can't remember Valentine's Day unless you tack a note to his forehead.
10. Needs a map to find the laundry hamper.

CD Holder

Trampoline

Refrigerator Magnet

Two Bonus Uses for an Ex
Who Makes Service Calls

1. Safe sex (strictly platonic and only for tension relief)
2. Sperm donor (should your new spouse's count be a trifle low)

Sperm Donor

Plunger

Lawn Sprinkler

Bonus Use—Handyman

Does your ex own a toolbox? A ladder? Work shoes? Use him to perform tricky household tasks like:

- Grouting the bathroom tiles
- Fixing a leaky faucet
- Dredging the cesspool
- Pedicures
- Spackling
- Hanging pictures
- Rewiring a lamp
- Removing a waterbug the size of Guam that happened to expire directly under your sink (show you care; lend him a pair of tweezers)
- Installing a ceiling fan
- Changing a fuse (if you're still angry, encourage him to perform this task while standing barefoot in a pail of water)

Hood Ornament

Ceiling Fan

Richard Smith

Bonus Use—Headhunter

Does your ex have lots of cute friends? If the marriage broke up
because he a) needed his space or b) was having an affair or c) had a
personality disorder (kept excusing himself during intimate moments
to go powder his nose), your ex-husband may be responsible for find-
ing you a new mate. (See Paragraph VII of your divorce agreement.)

Ski Rack

127

Laundry Hamper

In Case of Emergency:
12 Last-Minute Uses for an Ex

IF	RECOMMENDED USE
He has an extra-pointy nose	Drill bit
The river's flooding	Sandbag
He has a magnetic personality	Job site cleanup: Picking up bits of metal . . . paper clips, nails, iron shavings, tacks, etc.
He's chubby	Filling potholes
He's obese	Yucky Spam
He has love handles	Free weight
He looks kind of cute with a lit candle in his mouth	Jack-o'-lantern
He has a crew cut	Floor polisher
He has a prominent forehead	Smoothing unsightly bulges in newly applied wallpaper
He wears dentures	Guitar picks*
His feet are exceptionally flat	Tamping down new topsoil
He sucks	Vacuum cleaner

* Or paper shredder